Mysteries of the Universe

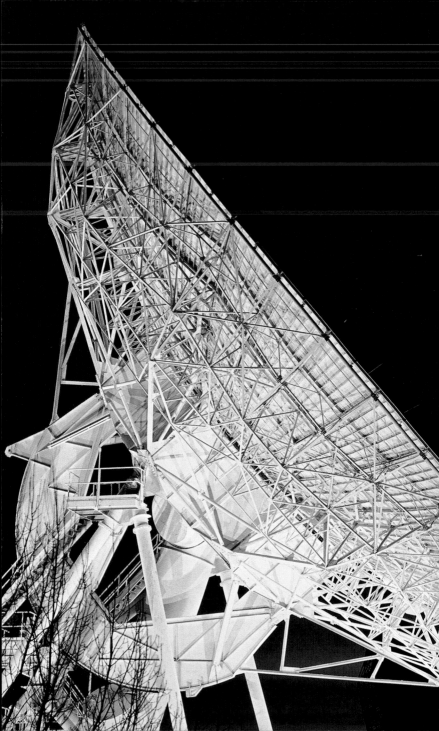

Mysteries *of* the Universe

How Astronomers Explore Space

By Andrew Einspruch

NATIONAL GEOGRAPHIC

WASHINGTON D.C.

One of the world's largest nonprofit scientific and educational organizations, the National Geographic Society was founded in 1888 "for the increase and diffusion of geographic knowledge." Fulfilling this mission, the Society educates and inspires millions every day through its magazines, books, television programs, videos, maps and atlases, research grants, the National Geographic Bee, teacher workshops, and innovative classroom materials. The Society is supported through membership dues, charitable gifts, and income from the sale of its educational products. This support is vital to National Geographic's mission to increase global understanding and promote conservation of our planet through exploration, research, and education.

For more information, please call
1-800-NGS-LINE (647-5463) or write to the following address:
National Geographic Society
1145 17th Street N.W.
Washington, D.C. 20036-4688
U.S.A.

For information about special discounts for bulk purchases, please contact
National Geographic Books Special Sales at ngspecsales@ngs.org

Visit the Society's Web site: www.nationalgeographic.com

Copyright © 2006 National Geographic Society

Text revised from *How We Learn About Space* in the National Geographic Windows on Literacy program from National Geographic School Publishing, © 2004 National Geographic Society

Published by National Geographic Society. Washington, D.C. 20036

Design by Project Design Company

Printed in the United States

Library of Congress
Cataloging-in-Publication Data

Einspruch, Andrew.
  Mysteries of the universe : how astronomers explore space / by Andrew Einspruch.
    p. cm. -- (National Geographic science chapters)
  Includes bibliographical references and index.
  ISBN-13: 978-0-7922-5956-5 (lib. binding)
  ISBN-10: 0-7922-5956-4 (lib. binding)
  1. Outer space--Exploration. I. Title. II. Series.
  QB500.262.E46 2006
  919.904--dc22

                         2006016331

Photo Credits

Front Cover: © PhotoDisc/ Getty Images; Spine: © Art Montes De Oca/ Taxi/ Getty Images; Endpaper: © Art Montes De Oca/ Taxi/ Getty Images; 2-3: © Carlos Casariego/ The Image Bank/ Getty Images; 6: © NASA; 8: © Photolibrary.com; 9: © PhotoDisc/ Getty Images; 10: © Richard Nowitz/ National Geographic/ Getty Images; 12, 13: NASA; 14: © APL/ Corbis; 15: © PhotoDisc/ Getty Images; 16, 17, 18, 19, 20, 21, 22, 23: © NASA; 24: © Photolibrary.com; 25, 27 (top): © NASA; 27 (bottom): © Digital Vision; 28: © APL/ Corbis; 29, 30, 31, 32: © NASA; 33 (top): © Photolibrary.com; 33 (bottom): NASA; 34: © PhotoDisc/ Getty Images.

An exploding star gives off
a cloud of gas and dust.

What's in Space?

Take a look at the night sky. What do you see? You might see the moon and some stars. You might even see a planet. People have always wanted to learn about things in the night sky.

There are lots of ways to learn about something. You can look at it closely. You can touch it. You can run tests. But how do you do this when the thing you want to learn about is millions of miles away?

People who study space are called astronomers. They have developed many different types of technology for learning about planets and stars and other mysteries of the universe.

An astronomer uses a giant telescope to look at objects in the night sky.

Chapter 1

Telescopes

One way to study space is to look at it. Using just your eyes, you can see many things in the night sky. You can see the moon, lots of stars, and some of the planets. Unfortunately, it's impossible to see any details. Stars, for instance, just look like specks of light. If you want a better look, you need to use a telescope. A telescope lets you look closely at things that are far away.

▶ With a small telescope you can see craters on the moon.

Giant radio telescopes in New Mexico collect radio signals from space.

Kinds of Telescopes

Optical telescopes collect light reflected by objects in space. Large optical telescopes are housed in buildings called observatories. The telescopes in observatories can gather light from stars millions of miles away.

Objects in space also give off radio waves. Radio telescopes are huge dish-shaped metal mirrors that collect radio signals from space. By studying these radio signals, astronomers have been able to measure the temperature of all the planets.

The Hubble Space Telescope

There can be problems with using telescopes on Earth. Clouds, dirty air, and city lights get in the way of seeing objects in space. To get around this problem, scientists built a space telescope.

The Hubble Space Telescope was sent into space in 1990. It orbits, or travels around, Earth. Hubble orbits about 350 miles (563 km) above Earth where there aren't any lights or dirty air.

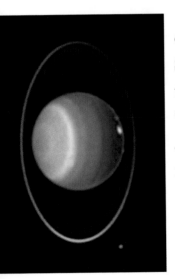

Hubble sends pictures of space back to Earth. Scientists have seen amazing things in these pictures. They saw a comet crash into Jupiter. They also discovered many small moons that circle Saturn and Uranus.

Images from Hubble show many bright clouds on the planet Uranus.

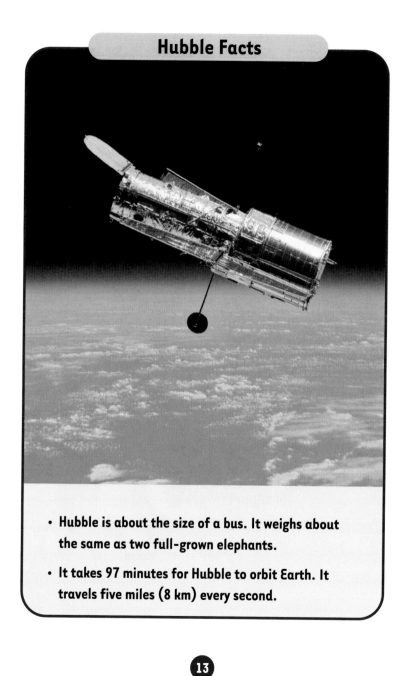

- Hubble is about the size of a bus. It weighs about the same as two full-grown elephants.

- It takes 97 minutes for Hubble to orbit Earth. It travels five miles (8 km) every second.

Chapter 2

Sending People Into Space

If you are curious about a country, you can read about it and look at pictures. But to find out what it is really like, you have to go there. It's the same with space. The best way to get to know it is to go there.

People started traveling into space in 1961. Yuri Gagarin, a Russian astronaut, was the first human to go into space. He orbited Earth once.

◀ A cable keeps an astronaut from floating away when he works in space.

▶ Yuri Gagarin went into space on April 12, 1961.

15

This rocket launched
astronauts into space.

The first spacecraft were blasted into space on powerful rockets. The rockets had to be strong enough to overcome gravity, the force that pulls things toward Earth. Early space missions were designed to learn about space travel. Astronauts who orbited Earth discovered what it was like to be in space without gravity.

John Glenn climbs into the spacecraft he rode in when he became the first American to orbit Earth.

Going to the Moon

The moon is the closest thing in space to Earth. It is much closer than the sun or the planets. Scientists sent astronauts to the moon so they could learn what it was like there.

Buzz Aldrin walked on the moon on July 20, 1969.

An astronaut drove the lunar rover on the moon.

Before going to the moon, American astronauts made ten trips into space. These flights tested ideas about getting to the moon and back. Finally, in 1969, two astronauts landed on the moon. Neil Armstrong and Edwin "Buzz" Aldrin collected moon rocks to examine back on Earth.

The last time people went to the moon was 1972. Two astronauts drove around in a moon car called a lunar rover. They were able to explore parts of the moon as far as 20 miles (32 km) from their landing site.

This painting shows how the Space Shuttle carries astronauts to and from the International Space Station.

Chapter 3

Space Stations

Space stations are places where people can live in space. Space stations orbit around Earth. Crews of astronauts live in space stations for many months at a time.

The first space station, Skylab, was launched in 1973. It orbited Earth for six years. The Russian space station, Mir, orbited Earth from 1986 to 2001.

▶ Most of the Skylab missions focused on the challenges of living in space.

Astronauts from different countries work in the ISS.

International Space Station

Sixteen countries worked together to create the International Space Station, or ISS. The first parts of the ISS were sent into space in 1998. A crew of three astronauts, two Russian and one American, moved into the International Space Station in 2000. Crews live in the ISS for approximately six months before they return to Earth.

The ISS was made in large pieces called modules. The modules were sent into space one at a time. Then they were put together there. Astronauts live in one of the modules. Another module houses a laboratory where scientific experiments are conducted.

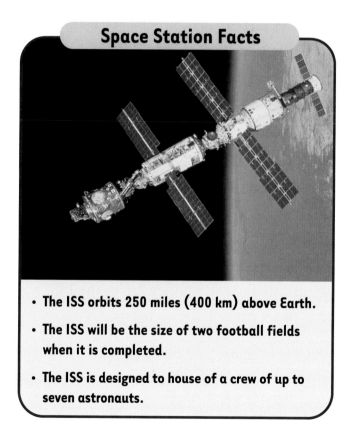

Space Station Facts

- The ISS orbits 250 miles (400 km) above Earth.

- The ISS will be the size of two football fields when it is completed.

- The ISS is designed to house of a crew of up to seven astronauts.

Living in Space

People in space need to
do the same everyday
things that you need to
do. They need to eat
and drink. They also
need to exercise their
bodies so that they
stay healthy.

▲ Food for the astronauts
is stored in packages.

Astronauts living in the space station eat
three meals every day. Some foods, like nuts
and fruit, are the same as we eat on Earth.
Other foods are dried so they weigh less and
can be stored longer. Foods are stored in
packages that hold enough for one meal.

Since there is no gravity in space,
astronauts float when they are in the ISS.
As a result, their muscles become weak. To
prevent this, all astronauts exercise for at
least one hour each day.

▶ This astronaut uses a machine to exercise his legs.

Science in Space

The International Space Station is a great place for science. Scientists on the ISS study how living things respond to being in a weightless environment for an extended period of time. For example, scientists look at what happens to people's bodies when they live in space. If astronauts don't exercise, they find it hard to walk when they get back to Earth.

Scientists also do experiments on plants in the space station. They look at how plants grow without gravity. This helps them figure out if astronauts will be able to grow their own food one day.

The information learned from experiments done on the ISS will help scientists plan future space missions. This kind of knowledge is vital if humans are to travel far from Earth to distant planets such as Mars.

▲ This scientist is doing an experiment to grow plants in space.

◄ Scientists on the ISS study Earth's weather.

This space probe flew by Saturn
and sent photos back to Earth.

Space Probes

Astronauts haven't been to the planets because they are so far away from Earth. So scientists send space probes to planets to get a closer look. Space probes are unmanned spacecraft. The first space probes were sent into space about fifty years ago. They were sent to the moon, Venus, and Mars. Since then, space probes have been sent to every planet.

Saturn

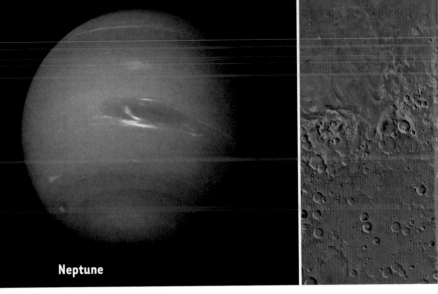

Neptune

Space probes took these photographs.

How Do Space Probes Work?

Most space probes fly by a planet. The probe takes photographs and gathers other data about the planet and its atmosphere. The probe then sends this information back to Earth.

Using space probes, scientists have seen lightning and storms on Jupiter. They have discovered that Saturn has over 1,000 rings. They have also seen pictures of clouds and storms on Neptune.

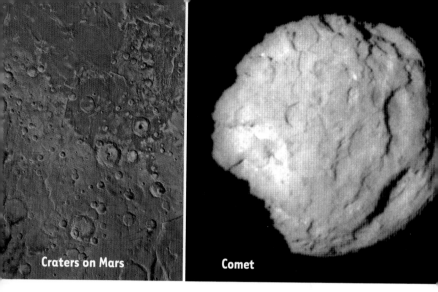

Craters on Mars

Comet

Not all space probes gather data about planets. Astronomers use some probes to learn about comets, asteroids, and other objects in space.

Space Probe Facts

It can take many years for a space probe to reach a distant planet.

Jupiter: 2 years

Uranus: 8.5 years

Saturn: 4 years

Neptune: 12 years

Exploring Mars

Some space probes land on a planet. In 2004, two space probes called rovers landed on Mars. The rovers, named Opportunity and Spirit, are robots on wheels. Each rover is about the size of a golf cart. For more than two years, the rovers have explored Mars and sent information back to Earth.

The rovers have each traveled more than four miles (6 km) across the Martian surface. They have taken thousands of color photographs. The pictures show the rocks, craters, and red soil on Mars. Tools on the rovers also help scientists study the rocks on Mars.

The images and data collected by the rovers show that there was once water on this dry, dusty planet. Finding evidence of water on Mars makes scientists wonder if there was life on this planet at one time.

▲ An artist's model shows
what the rover looked like
as it roamed across Mars.

◀ A photo taken by one of the
rovers shows the planet's
red, rocky surface.

Looking Ahead

We know a lot about space, but there is much more to learn. Astronomers have many ideas. Some scientists want to set up a space colony on the moon or send people to Mars. Other astronomers are more interested in studying stars and want to send probes to faraway galaxies. One thing is certain. People will always look up into the night sky and want to know more about what's out there. They will continue to want to unlock the mysteries of the universe.

People use telescopes to get a better look at the stars and other objects in space.

How to Write an A+ Report

1. Choose a topic.
- Find something that interests you.
- Make sure it is not too big or too small.

2. Find sources.
- Ask your librarian for help.
- Use many different sources: books, magazine articles, and websites.

3. Gather information.
- Take notes. Write down the big ideas and interesting details.
- Use your own words.

4. Organize information.
- Sort your notes into groups that make sense.

- Make an outline. Put your groups of notes in the order you want to write your report.

5. Write your report.

- Write an introduction that tells what the report is about.

- Use your outline and notes as you write to make sure you say everything you want to say in the order you want to say it.

- Write an ending that tells about your report.

- Write a title.

6. Revise and edit your report.

- Read your report to make sure it makes sense.

- Read it again to check spelling, punctuation, and grammar.

7. Hand in your report!

asteroid	a small, rocky object that travels around the sun
astronaut	a person trained to fly a spacecraft
astronomer	a person who studies space
comet	a ball of ice with a long tail of gas that travels around the sun
galaxy	a group of stars and planets
gravity	a force that pulls things toward Earth
laboratory	a place where experiments are done
module	a part that fits with other parts to make something
observatory	a building with a powerful telescope for observing the sky
orbit	to travel in a curved path around a planet or star
radio telescope	an instrument that collects radio signals from space
space probe	unmanned spacecraft that travels in space to collect information about space and send it back to Earth
space station	a spacecraft in which a crew lives in space for an extended period of time
telescope	an instrument that makes distant objects look closer and bigger
universe	everything that exists in space

Further Reading

• Books •

Apt, Jay, Michael Helfert, and Justin Wilkinson. *Orbit: NASA Astronauts Photograph the Earth*. Washington, DC: National Geographic Society, 2003. Grades 7-12, 224 pages.

Constellations (First Pocket Guide Series). Washington, DC: National Geographic Society, 2002. Ages 8-10, 80 pages.

Dyson, Marianne J. *Home on the Moon: Living on a Space Frontier*. Washington, DC: National Geographic Society, 2003. Ages 9-12, 64 pages.

Skurzynski, Gloria. *Are We Alone? Scientists Search for Life in Space*. Washington, DC: National Geographic Society, 2004. Ages 9-12, 96 pages.

Skurzynski, Gloria. *Discovering Mars*. Washington, DC: National Geographic Society, 1998. Ages 9-12, 48 pages.

Stars and Planets (First Pocket Guide Series). Washington, DC: National Geographic Society, 2002. Ages 8-10, 80 pages.

• Websites •

AeroSpaceGuide
http://www.aerospaceguide.net/space_kids.html

History of Space Exploration
http://www.solarviews.com/eng/history.htm

HubbleSite
http://hubblesite.org/

National Aeronautics and Space Administration
http://education.nasa.gov/home/index.html

Sea and Sky
http://www.seasky.org/sky5.html

Wikipedia Online Encyclopedia
http://en.wikipedia.org/wiki/Space_exploration

Index